59345321R00084

Made in the USA
Middletown, DE
10 August 2019